Robbery Under Arms

Dark Days on the Highways

Through the gullies and creeks they rode silently down;
They stuck-up the station and raided the town;
They opened the safe and they looted the bank;
They laughed and were merry, they ate and they drank;
Then off to the ranges they went with their gold—
Oh! Never were bandits more reckless and bold.

THE BUSHRANGERS — EDWARD HARRINGTON

GEOFF HOCKING

Contents

front cover:
A Bush Hold-up
(drawing by William Strutt) National Library of Australia, an3212003

title page:
Capture of Bushrangers at Night by Gold Police
(watercolour by George Lacy) Rex Nan Kivell Collection, R4113. National Library of Australia, an3103554

left: Theatre Poster, Theatre Royal, Tasmania, 1896
J. W. B. Murphy Collection, Tasmaniana Library, State Library of Tasmania

Robbery Under Arms

Victoria had attracted the refuse of the adjoining penal settlement of Van Diemen's Land, herded together and ... ready to undertake any crime.

— McCombie Australian Sketches

The Second Generation – The Scourge of the Settlers

WITH THE DEMISE OF THE LAST OF THE convict outlaws 'Bold' John Donohoe, or 'The Wild Colonial Boy', the governors of the eastern colonies were satisfied that they had put an end at last to the era of bushranging. The bands of desperate runaways had all been rounded up, imprisoned or executed.

Or so the governors thought.

While there may have been a few years of relative peace in the colonies, the end to **transportation**, the release and **emancipation** of the convict classes, the emigration of free workers into the rural and emerging manufacturing economy, and the arrival of ship-loads of young women eager to settle into the adventure of colonial life, saw a dramatic shift in the colonial power base.

The common man was feeling his strength and demanding his place under the sun. No longer were the working classes prepared to sit back and let the squatters and the politicians (quite often the same people) have it all. The people demanded a fair go, but they weren't going to get it without a long and bitter struggle.

The discovery of gold in 1851 made revolutionary changes to the opportunities available to all who cared to work at it, and the world was soon turned 'topsy-turvy'.

There were those who could not wait for that bonanza on a distant horizon. Many of these people were convicts or ex-convicts who had had enough of hard labour and still looked for the easy way out of their misery. They were the ones who took to the roads in search of 'their share'. When the roads were teeming with lucky diggers, their pockets filled with nuggets, they took those as well.

—Prisoner of the 'Crown'—

IN 1838, A SKULL HAD BEEN UNEARTHED in a creek in central Victoria in the area now known as Castlemaine. It was dug up by some natives, and Captain John Hepburn — one of the first squatters to pass through the region — came upon the skull lying in the sand. Hepburn recalled:

> 'On the brink of a waterhole at the junction of the creeks … I buried the skull of a prisoner of the Crown who was murdered by his mates after absconding. It was dug up by the natives twice, and the third time I buried it in the dry deposit in the waterhole.'

It appears that the skull was part of the remains of a group of escaped convicts, including George Comerford and Joseph Dignum, who, with six others, bolted from a work party near Yass. They made their way towards Melbourne, planning their escape to South Australia, attacking settlers and homesteads on their way south.

Tiring of his bickering companions, Comerford decided to go it alone. He waited until they fell asleep and rose with an axe in hand; Dignum, who must have had the same idea, rose as well. They killed the others as they slept, and threw their bodies onto the campfire.

The next day Comerford and Dignum set off for Melbourne. They worked for a while for a squatter they had met on the way, but they had bigger fish to fry. As they left their employment unannounced, the squatter had a warrant issued for their arrest. Before they could be brought to trial they broke away again, taking some **muskets** with them.

Comerford and Dignum went on a bushranging spree before they headed once again for South Australia. This time it was Dignum who decided that he would be better off alone, so he took a shot at Comerford. He missed, and Comerford scurried off, heading back to Melbourne. Hoping to save his own neck, Comerford turned Queen's evidence against his old friend Dignum and the pair were eventually brought to trial. Nobody believed Comerford's story about the campfire by the Castlemaine creek, so he was taken back into the district to prove his account.

The police who escorted Comerford back to the foothills of Mt. Alexander were shocked to discover that his account was true; bones, skulls and blackened clothing were still sticking out of the ashes of the long-cold fire.

On the way back to Melbourne, Comerford escaped again. After snatching the **carbine** of one policeman, Comerford turned and killed him. Once again George Comerford was at large. He returned to his old tricks, and eventually a reward of £50 was offered for his capture. A convict hut-keeper named Kangaroo Jack recognised Comerford on a cattle station just out of town. As Comerford settled down in front of the fire and proceeded to light his pipe, Kangaroo Jack belted him over the head, knocking him to the floor. Comerford was soon set upon by others in the hut, then bound and carted away once again to face the judge.

To make sure that Comerford didn't escape again, the judge ordered that he be taken away and hanged by the neck until dead. Dignum escaped the ultimate penalty, sentenced to only seven years for his part in the murder of seven convicts. George Comerford died on the gallows for the murder of one policeman. Who says that British justice isn't fair?

E.J.HARTY, LITH. 9, DAME ST DUBLIN.

THE REFORMED EXILES

Dark Roads to the Diggings

IN 1851, GOLD WAS DISCOVERED near Bathurst in New South Wales. In September of the same year, gold was discovered in the central highlands of Victoria.

Within months of these discoveries, thousands of eager gold-seekers rushed into the goldfields from across the border, across Bass Strait and from across the seas. At one time there were so many ships left crewless in Port Phillip Bay that the scene resembled a European pine forest.

Among the thousands of hopeful 'new chums' were the old lags: the escapees from the **chain gangs** and work parties who had found their way across Bass Strait with the sealers and whalers.

The **'vandemonians'** were the most feared of all in the new colony. These men, and some women,

had been brutalised by the lash and **triangle**, and seen all manner of deprivation and degradation. Hardened criminals, they had little time for the niceties of the civilisation that they had left behind them so long ago when they were first trundled aboard the prison ships in England.

Lord Robert Cecil wrote in his journal following a trip to the central Victorian diggings that:

'Mr Latrobe [the Governor] told me that no fewer than 400 were missing from Van Diemen's Land, and were doubtless at the diggings.'

Lord Cecil continues in his diary:

'These men, though bad characters, have a wholesome respect for the law from having been experimentally made acquainted with its terrors; and they dare not brave it openly.'

It was a common practice for bushrangers to ask travellers on the road whether they were

5

Black Douglas

BLACK DOUGLAS was a **mulatto** Indian who began his bushranging career around the Maryborough region in central Victoria. He later moved operations to the Black Forest on the road between Melbourne and Bendigo.

Hundreds of diggers made their way up and down this road daily, and every one of them was aware of the dangers that lurked within that darkened forest of close-growing tall trees and thick scrub. Tracks wound all over the forest floor, and the unwary traveller could easily lose his way, his possessions or his life.

There are many records of confrontations with Black Douglas, or there are at least countless references to him in diaries and recollections of adventures on the diggings. The name 'Black Douglas' was the most feared of all. It was the one name that all travellers were warned of before they set off for the goldfields.

He pops up time and again:

'I saw at one time 16 … poor fellows fastened to a log with that notorious robber, Black Douglas …'

So wrote Henry Leversha in a letter to the Castlemaine Pioneers in 1880, when describing licence defaulters chained 'to the logs' at the Castlemaine Police Camp.

A Polish migrant, Seweryn Korzelinksi, who had a shop on the Alma goldfield near Maryborough, recalled that Black Douglas and his band of thieves had made their headquarters only three miles away. While they pretended to work at gold-digging, their main occupation was stealing from tents and shops. This was an easy sort of robbing as the tents were empty during the day and the shops were empty at night:

'The method was to organise a fight late at night in the vicinity of the front of the shop, and when the merchant came out curious to see the fisticuffs, accomplices would cut the canvas wall at the rear and grab what they could.'

Korzelinski recalled the capture of Black Douglas when the diggers, fed up with the thieves, surrounded their tents one night, tied the robbers up and burnt the tents to the ground. Douglas, who was a huge and powerful man, fought hardest until he was wounded, and then able to be overpowered. He was carted to Maryborough with an escort of more than 200 miners.

Korzelinski says that he was taken to Melbourne and hanged, but there is no record today that confirms the demise of Black Douglas.

GOLD LEVIED WITHOUT LICENSE.

Engraving by S. T. Gill.
From John Sherer The Gold Finder in Australia, *published in 1853.*

'going up' or 'coming down'. Wayfarers were in greater danger if they answered 'coming down' as it would be assumed that they carried gold receipts, cheques or money with them:

'It was not an uncommon thing in those days for "road agents" to take into the bush anyone who had gold receipts or cheques, bind him to a tree and place a **sentinel** over him, and then despatch one of their number to Melbourne either to cash the cheque or to get possession of the gold by giving up the receipt …'

So wrote gold-digger William Craig who travelled the roads to Bendigo and Ballarat in the 1850s. He also wrote:

'A little before noon we sighted a spring-cart *en route* for Melbourne, in which were seated a man and a woman who informed us they had come from Ballarat, and had been bailed up at their camp the previous night by five men … the robbers had taken from them about five pounds' weight of gold, and what money and valuables they possessed, with the exception of an old silver watch …'

Craig records that the woman had recovered her treasured keepsake from the top branch of a tall tree where one of the villains had placed it after she had 'roundly abused them'. She refused to give up her watch as it was a gift from a near relative, given to her before she had left the 'old country'.

Craig felt the woman had been quite forthright with the bushrangers in expressing her demands, she had said that she had been in the colonies for several years and was not ready to give in so easily. Curiously enough, the villains did leave her this prized possession – just that it was at the top of a tree – and 'she might have it if she cared to climb for it'.

There was one name that was on every digger's lips as he set off for the diggings – 'Black Douglas', Craig wrote:

'Before we started next morning we heard of bushrangers, Black Douglas and his men were about, and as the majority of us were armed we felt particularly plucky, but as we would not know a bushranger if we saw him we suspected everybody … I really think that if anyone had looked black at us we would have done a bit of shooting, but if, on the other hand, a revolver had been pointed at us, I have my doubts of the pluck holding out.'

'Everyone had to go armed as there was so much sticking-up and horse stealing. Many a poor fellow had been put out of the way during those times, and never heard of any more. It was every man for himself.'

'We unloaded, and returned to a place called the Devil's Elbow, where we camped. A man rode up, and after fastening his horse came towards my cousin. Suspicions were aroused, so he went towards his dray and got underneath. I stood by the fire and had an axe in my hand. He came towards me, asked me for a drink, at the same time pulling a bottle from his coat pocket. As his coat lifted, I saw two revolvers stuck in his belt. I declined, as I saw his object was to get us together and then he would have stuck us up …'

Then, later, back on the road to Bendigo …

'One night as I came through the Black Forest, two men suddenly sprang out from the bushes, and sang out for me to stop. I had between £60 and £70 in my pocket. My horses were fresh and lively, and I slashed my whip around them in a moment, and if the men had not jumped out of the way, my cart would have dashed over them; thus I saved myself from being robbed …'

Melbourne 1855, as seen from the north, near the road to Mt. Alexander (lithograph by Henry Burn, 1855)
La Trobe Picture Collection, State Library of Victoria

Bushrangers Waiting for the Mails in New South Wales (watercolour by S.T. Gill, c. 1851)
La Trobe Picture Collection, State Library of Victoria

Diggers Attacked on the Mt. Alexander Road

John Flanigan and Thomas Williams were among a party of bushrangers who were active across the roads to the goldfields. At Flanigan's trial for the stick-up at Aitken's Gap, just north of Melbourne, his guilt was confirmed when one of the diggers he had robbed claimed the pistol found on Flanigan as his own.

Anthony Waring proved that the 'A.W.' carved on the stock of the gun was most assuredly him and not the initials of the captive John Flanigan (whose real name was Owen Gibney — born in Dublin and transported to Van Diemen's Land in 1842 for seven years for the crime of highway robbery).

It seems that even after a decade on the roads and several years in irons, Flanigan had not had enough of the highways. He was back in court again for playing the same old game.

Flanigan spent his next 10 years inside the floating hulks in Hobson's Bay. There were no roads there for him to roam.

'Bushrangers stick up returning diggers, tie them to trees, rob them of their gold, whether concealed in belts or boots. This plunder they spend in debauchery.'

'Whilst we were camped in the Black Forest … some highwaymen slit our tent with the intention of robbing us, but the men who were camped along with us heard the would-be depredators and immediately opened fire on them. Our visitors took to their horses and made off, firing back at us as they galloped away …'

There were any number of bandits who caused concern on the roads to and from all of the goldfields both in Victoria and New South Wales. There are some familiar and famous names among them – Captain Melville, Captain Moonlite, Captain Thunderbolt – to name but the most adventurous of them all. However, there were also plenty of others whose selection of witty nickname was not as exciting as these three grand 'gentlemen of the highways'.

— THE ROBBERY OF THE *NELSON* —

UNDER COVER OF DARKNESS on 2 April 1852, a number of men took two boats from Mr Liardet's mooring at Sandridge Pier and rowed out to the brig *Nelson* anchored two miles out in Port Phillip Bay.

The bulk of the crew had run for the diggings, leaving only a few sailors and passengers aboard that night. They were asleep in their bunks when they were awoken by shouts from the upper-deck. As each man came upon the deck to see what the fuss was all about, he was immediately grabbed by the intruders and tied to the **bulwark**.

The *Nelson* had just been loaded with £25,000 worth of gold; 8,000 ounces in 23 boxes had been ferried ashore during the day.

The mate-in-charge refused to show his attackers where the gold was stashed, and received a shot in his side and a few pokes with a sword as further encouragement. Fearing that he would be killed, he gave in and showed the 'pirates' to the strongroom.

The robbers broke down the door and carried the boxes out onto the deck. Locking all those aboard inside the strongroom, they nailed the door shut. The robbers lowered the gold into Liardet's boats, headed back for the shore and buried the loot in the sand to be recovered the next day.

A reward was offered for the capture of any of the men who had taken part in the daring and most lucrative robbery. For capture and conviction £250 was offered, and a further £500 from the **consignors** of the gold, Jackson, Rae & Co.

Before long, some familiar old felons were taken into custody — all 'vandemonians' — John James, transportee 15 years VDL; James Morgan, transportee 15 years VDL; James Duncan, stonemason free on arrival in the colony but took to bushranging around the Black Forest area at the beginning of the gold rushes; and Stephen Fox, transportee.

There were inconsistencies in the reported account of this black night: some said there were seven or eight bandits, others estimated as many as 25, while some were convinced there were only four.

At the Geelong Court on 29 June 1852, Duncan, James, Morgan and Fox were each sentenced to 15 years on the roads.

Daylight Robbery on St. Kilda Road

The *Argus*, 18 October 1852

BUSHRANGERS ON THE ST. KILDA ROAD:—

On Saturday night information was given at the Police station that four mounted and armed bushrangers were committing the most daring depredations on the St. Kilda and Brighton Road. About five o'clock in the evening, Mr and Mrs Bawfree were stopped, bailed up, and robbed, and upwards of fifteen other persons were also stopped that evening by the same gang.

A watch was then kept up and down the road, and every individual who came up on foot, or horseback, or in a vehicle, for two hours and a half, was stopped, and robbed.

THIS DARING DAYLIGHT ROBBERY certainly captured the attention of the citizens of Port Phillip. They may have been aware of the bandits in the bush, but they certainly didn't expect them in the town. While the St. Kilda to Brighton Road was, at that time, still in open country, influential citizens had

Strutt, William (1825–1915). Bushrangers, Victoria, Australia 1852, (1887), oil on canvas 75.7cm (H) x 156.6cm (W). The University of Melbourne Art Collection. Gift of Russell and Mab Grimwade Bequest 1973. 1973.0038.000.000

already begun to establish properties south of the river and surrounding the bay, and they were ripe for picking.

When John Flanigan, Thomas Williams and three others bailed up, they created the sort of fuss that had the media buzzing. John Sherer wrote in his book *The Gold-Finder in Australia*, published in 1853:

'On Saturday afternoon, about half-past three o'clock of a bright sunny day, two residents of Brighton – W. Keel and W. Robinson – were driving in a cart along the high road leading past the St. Kilda Racecourse leading to the special survey. Two men were walking before them at a little distance. They saw two or three other men, with guns at their sides, apparently looking up into the trees for birds. On a sudden they found themselves surrounded, guns were placed at their heads, and at that of the horse; and they were ordered to dismount.

The attack was so outrageous that they thought it was a joke; but as they were addressed in the most abusive language, and told that their brains would be blown out if they delayed, they got out of the cart and submitted to be rifled ...' One of these men lost £23 and the other £46 before they were both ordered into a wattle scrub, tied hand to hand and forced to sit on the ground. What an indignity!

The two men that they had just passed on the road were brought in to join them, robbed, tied, bound and also on the ground. For the next hour and a half every individual on foot, horseback or vehicle suffered the same indignity. There were now 27 hapless citizens lined up in the wattle beside the St. Kilda Road. When a Mr and Mrs Bawtree came along the road in their jaunty gig, they too were manhandled into the bush. Bawtree demanded that his wife not be subjected to a search. One of the bushrangers shouted at him with the vilest of bad language that he would have his brains blown out if he didn't move along pretty smartly. As this couple was being forced to the ground, one raider instructed another to 'put them all together, so that if you miss one, you will kill another'.

A gentleman on horseback came trotting down the road. He too was called to surrender, but he dug his spurs deeply into the flanks of his mount and galloped off. Two shots were fired after him as cries of murder were heard from the bush. One of the bushrangers, apparently worse for the liquor, started to become very loud and aggressive, when one of the others angrily advised him: 'You had better be quiet; there has been one man shot already. I should not like to shoot another.'

The *Argus* newspaper report of the incident continued:

'At sundown the bushrangers drew off the man acting as guard, and shortly afterwards the sound of horse's feet was heard galloping off through the bush apparently in the direction of South Yarra. They [the victims] then liberated themselves, and proceeded to their residences.'

A £2,000 reward for information leading to the capture of the 'five armed bushrangers' was offered on 19 October. Police apprehended two men in Flinders Lane just after the reward had been posted. Some policemen had approached two suspicious-looking horsemen just after midnight. When they were unable to give a satisfactory reply to the officers' questions they were taken into custody. The horsemen were none other than John Flanigan and Thomas Williams, who were responsible for a hold-up at Aitken's

Gap on the Mt. Alexander Road earlier that same day.

Flanigan was carrying £47, Williams £55 in notes and sovereigns, and a small nugget. Williams also had a bundle of clothing and two 'chooks' trussed up ready for their dinner. Both had with them a pair of loaded pistols.

At their trial, a pistol stolen at Aitken's Gap was used in evidence against Flanigan. Victims of the earlier robbery at St. Kilda were also called as witnesses, and they all remembered the pair who had so sorely interrupted their journey along the St. Kilda to Brighton Road.

Flanigan and Williams were both sentenced to 30 years imprisonment for their jaunt south of the Yarra.

Williams later paid the ultimate price, going to his death on the gallows for his part in the brutal murder of Inspector-General John Price at the Gellibrand quarries in March 1854.

Study for Bushrangers on the St. Kilda Road (drawing by William Strutt, 1886)
La Trobe Picture Collection, State Library of Victoria

*Lake Albert Mounted Police Chasing Bushrangers,
Overland from Port Phillip to South Australia
(watercolour by S. T. Gill, c. 1840)*

Morgan Sticking up the Navvies, Turning Their Tents and Shooting the Chinaman, 1865

Francis McCallum — 'Captain Melville'

FRANK McCALLUM – alias 'Captain Melville' – was one bushranger who seemed to have a split personality. He was, on the one hand, a charmer, polite and gallant especially where the ladies were concerned; on the other hand, he could turn, in an instant, to unseemly brutality.

McCallum had been transported to Van Diemen's Land in 1838 at the age of 12. He was one of the 'boy convicts' who were sent out to the colony at the time when there was a repeated push for an end to transportation, and 'free' labour was becoming scarce.

The government thought that boys would pose no threat, so they rounded up 150 petty thieves and pickpockets. Prison was no reform home: it simply served to debase the juveniles at the pleasure of the old lags.

It is a surprise that young Frank had turned out so well at all. He arrived in Port Phillip in late 1851, intending to look for gold, but like so many other 'vandemonians' he too tried to get it the easy way.

William Craig met Captain Melville when he visited Cartwright's home-station at Sailor Creek to purchase his weekly provisions. As he came towards the property, he observed a well-cared-for horse tethered to the front fence of the house. Thinking it must have been the horse of a government official, Craig lifted the latch and entered the kitchen where he was surprised to be staring into the barrel of a revolver:

'I found myself facing a revolver and was ordered in a peremptory way to throw up my hands … my facial aspect, and perhaps my then somewhat dilapidated 'new chum' clothing,

Melville's Caves

Rumours have it that 'Captain Melville' had stashed his ill-gotten gains somewhere in the many caves that riddle a granite outcrop at Mt. Kooyoora, near Inglewood, on the central north-eastern Victorian goldfields.

Melville would retreat into his fastness in these hills after a raid, and the police could never get near him.

As William Craig had observed, Melville had developed a unique relationship with his horse Bob. Bob was as good as any watchdog, alerting Melville of the arrival of any inter-lopers that may have placed his gentle master in jeopardy.

It is a pity, for Melville, that his horse Bob was not allowed into that brothel in Geelong on that fateful day.

afforded him considerable amusement, and with a loud hearty laugh he lowered the weapon and ordered me to [sit].'

Melville had been eating when Craig walked through the door. After he was satisfied that Craig was no threat he continued with his meal. Craig observed that he was well-dressed and ate with refinement. Melville's language was polite and without blasphemy, but when he heard a footfall on the verandah step, he swung about as quick as lightning and his revolver was once again covering another poor digger as he stepped into the room. Melville asked the digger if he had any money, and when he replied that he had only a few shillings, Melville gave him one pound and a few shillings from his pocket, half of what he had himself. He said, 'Well, old man. I'm Melville the outlaw – you've doubtless heard of me. I'm not flush of loose cash just now, but I'll share what I have with you.'

Craig also observed the way in which Melville treated his horse. When the horse heard his master approaching, he whinnied with pleasure; Melville fondled and whispered to the beast, and the horse responded, rubbing his nose against the outlaw's face and shoulders. Swinging up onto his mount, his rifle slung across his shoulders, Melville lightly touched the horse's flanks and disappeared into the Bullarook Forest.

After taking £33 from travellers Wearne and Madden on the road to Geelong, he handed back £10 as it was so close to Christmas he didn't want to spoil the holiday they were planning when they got there. Melville was heading that way himself. That holiday was to prove his undoing. With his mate, William Roberts, they continued down the road, sticking-up and stealing from everyone they met on their way.

It had been a long and lonely time on the road, and they began their festivities with a trip to a house of ill-fame. After a while, Roberts, a little worse for liquor, couldn't stop himself from boasting to the girl he was with. He declared himself to be a bushranger – in the company of 'Captain Melville'.

The lass slipped away at the first opportunity and summoned the police. Melville tried to escape by knocking one of the policemen off his horse, but he was not successful in gaining his freedom.

Tried and convicted in February 1853, the 'Captain' was sentenced to the hulks at Williamstown. Now aged 30, Frank McCallum was again imprisoned; this time the hulk *Success* was to be his floating hell for the next 32 years.

McCallum wasn't at all fond of prison life. He began this sentence attacking a warder and threatening to bite off his nose. For this he was flogged and spent the next 20 days in solitary confinement.

Each day the convicts were taken ashore in launches, where they laboured in the construction of wharves and other buildings around the bay. Some worked breaking stones at the Gellibrand quarries. McCallum was aboard one boat when nine of the convicts seized the tow rope and attacked the guard, throwing him overboard. The owner of the boat refused to leave, and he was brained by one of the other prisoners with his stone-breaking hammer. Shots were fired at them from the *Success,* killing one of the rioters. Melville and the murderous crew headed off down Hobson's Bay, making for a schooner they planned to seize to make their escape from Port Phillip.

The sentinel on the hulk had signalled to the shore, and a police launch set off, taking the bolters into custody again. Now heavily chained, they were cast back into their cells.

McCallum received the death penalty, but as **the Crown** could not show a warrant for his being removed from one boat to another he was spared on a technicality. His sentence was commuted to life imprisonment. After a glorious life on the diggings — dressed in the flashest of clothes, astride a gleaming steed, the ladies at his feet — the prospect of spending the rest of his miserable days aboard a rotting hulk must have proved too much for him.

Melville became his own executioner, choking himself with a handkerchief in August 1857. Roberts had also been sentenced to 32 years, in the hulk *President*. He was released in 1864.

Chinese Stick-em-ups!

There were some incidents during which some of the thousands of Chinese who came to the diggings took to the roads. A large and stout Chinese man held up a Mr Ball of Cathcart in New South Wales in 1859. Ball chased the man with his bull-whip, and he ran away.

Chinese laundry-man, Sam Poo, was one of the unlucky ones. Giving the laundry business away, he bailed up several people in the Mudgee district, but he shot the policeman who went to arrest him. He soon faced the same **retribution** as his European brothers-in-arms, and had his neck stretched on the gallows.

Attacking the Mail, Bushranging, NSW
(from a drawing by S. T. Gill, 1864)
National Library of Australia Collection, an7149198

Robbery on the Roads

IN JULY 1853, four enterprising American gentlemen arrived in the Colony of Victoria with the intention of establishing a coaching business that would service the Victorian goldfields. The first coaches ran between Melbourne and Castlemaine, the closest diggings to Port Phillip at that time.

By 1862 they had moved the centre of their operations to Bathurst, the oldest inland settlement in Australia at the heart of the New South Wales goldfields. Before the end of the century, Cobb & Co. had coaches running all over the country.

Although Cobb & Co. coaches ran across Australia for almost 80 years, ceasing its last Queensland operations in 1929, there were surprisingly few hold-ups. But those who faced the barrels of the bandits' guns certainly made the news of their day.

Cobb & Co.'s coaches were held up 36 times. There was a period when hold-ups were more frequent than others. In the years 1862 and 1863, coaches around Forbes and Bathurst in central New South Wales were attacked by bushrangers on at least nine occasions.

Attacks had become so frequent that a special commissioner was appointed to try the accused felons in Sydney in February 1863. On 10 February, three men were sentenced to be hanged on the one day, five more sentenced to 15 years hard labour, one to ten years and another to 12 years.

At times, the attackers did not have it all their own way. Sometimes passengers fought back. On 20 April 1868, bank manager Mr R. D. White fought back against five armed attackers who had bailed up the Gympie coach. He escaped by leaping from the coach and hiding in the bush beside the track.

On 6 January the following year, the Reverend G. E. King and another very brave bank manager, Mr W. E. King, also resisted an attack on the coach in which they were riding, wounding their attackers in their defence. Although the bandits still managed to abscond with £25, one was captured and sentenced to 20 years for his crime.

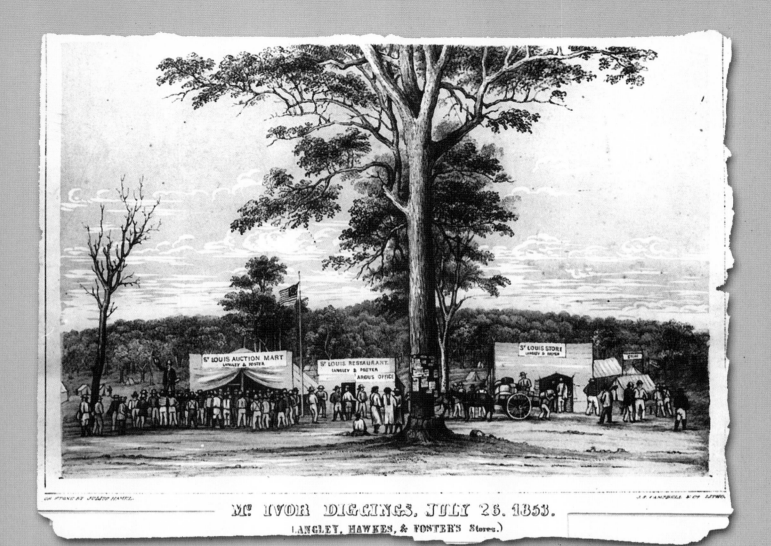

MC IVOR DIGGINGS. JULY 25. 1853.
(LANGLEY, HAWKES, & FOSTER'S Stores.)

The McIvor Escort Robbery, 20 July 1853

ON 20 JULY 1853, a large gang of bush-rangers attacked the Melbourne Gold Escort Company as it was carrying gold and mail from the McIvor (Heathcote) diggings en route to Kyneton where it was to meet up with the convoy from Bendigo.

As the dray turned a bend in the road, the driver was forced to swing around a large tree that was fallen across his way. As the troopers came closer to the tree, the superintendent became suspicious and called the escort to a halt.

Two men were hidden behind the fallen trunk and immediately opened fire. The troopers were also greeted with a volley of shots that rang out from an 'Aboriginal-style shelter' that had been thrown up beside the road. The driver of the dray was killed and several officers were wounded; they turned tail and fled in the middle of a sustained attack. Approximately 2,230 ounces of gold lay ripe for the picking.

The superintendent had dashed through the barricade and galloped off to the nearest police station where he raised the alarm. The other troopers had headed back to McIvor. On Monday 23 July, a reward was posted:

£250 for the apprehension and conviction of the parties who robbed the McIvor branch of the escort … and a further sum of £250 for the recovery of the stolen property, or a proportional sum, for the recovery of part thereof.

It wasn't long at all before most of the gang was apprehended attempting to leave the colony. There were so many characters with a past spent in chains in the community that any felon would have little chance of hiding his identity among them all. Generous rewards often brought speedy arrests.

Only £2,501/10s. in gold, notes, sovereigns and bankdrafts were recovered. Most of the booty was suspected to have already left the country. Some of those responsible for the daring daylight raid committed suicide before they were brought to justice. Three were hanged.

It is believed that Gray, the leader of the gang, was one of a large number of ruffians on board the *Madagascar*, which was lying in Hobson's Bay,

A Grisly End for George

After the McIvor Escort robbery, and while all of the rest of the gang had gone to Melbourne by various routes, one of two brothers, George Francis, returned to McIvor. As he could not account for his whereabouts on the day of the robbery, he was placed under arrest. He confessed all. But on his way to Melbourne for trial, George became so distressed that he had betrayed his mates, especially his brother, that he got hold of a razor and slit his throat from ear to ear.

ATTACK ON THE GOLD ESCORT BETWEEN McIVOR AND MELBOURNE.

ready for sea, at the time of the robbery. One of the others, George Wilson, had already paid for his ticket on the *Madagascar*, but it was his fondness for strong liquor that also saw him captured. He was safely aboard the ship when the police searched the vessel for ticket-of-leave men. Narrowly avoiding discovery, Wilson thought the coast was clear and decided to have a few drinks, but he had a few too many.

He was playing cards when he drew his revolver and threatened to shoot his playing companion. Wilson was placed under arrest. Fearing that one of his mates must have turned traitor, he too confessed everything, then instructed the officer to pull in alongside a ship making ready to sail to Mauritius. Once on deck, Wilson inquired if a George Melville (not to be confused with Captain Melville) was aboard, and to everyone's surprise Melville appeared. The police had been looking for him on another charge and were more than pleased to see him.

William Atkins, George Wilson and George Melville paid for their assault on the gold escort – they were hanged before a huge crowd on 3 October 1853. It took so long for George Melville to expire that the hangman had to pull down on his legs with 'considerable force before life was extinct'. Melville's widow took his corpse away to be displayed in the window of an oyster shop in Bourke Street, Melbourne, where it must have been an interesting advertising gimmick. After this display, all bodies of executed felons were buried within prison walls.

The *Madagascar* sailed away and was never heard of again. She had on board £60,000 of gold and a large number of homeward-bound diggers who had made their fortunes on the goldfields. There were also a large number of hardened felons and ticket-of-leave men whose appearance on board should have made the captain quake in his boots. It is believed that some of the *Nelson* robbers were also on board.

Rumours circulated for many years about what may have happened to the ship. Some suggested that the ship headed for Patagonia where the gold was put into long-boats and, as it was ferried ashore, the ship was sunk by bandits who, after throwing all of the passengers overboard, drilled holes in the hull. Others rumoured that the ship caught fire and all aboard perished, or that it hit an iceberg.

Gray, the leader of the McIvor Escort robbery, was never heard of again.

A Bush Hold-up, (drawing by William Strutt, c. 1855)
National Library of Australia Collection, an3212003

19

Conveying Gold from the Diggings to Melbourne. The Government Escort. 1851.

William Strutt del.

The Ballarat Bank Robbery

ALTHOUGH 'TICKET-OF-LEAVE' meant that ex-convicts were free to work, making their own way in the colony, they were expected to remain within the boundaries of the district indicated on their ticket. Few did.

When the water police inspected the *Nelson* and the *Madagascar* looking for the gold thieves, they were, primarily, looking for ticket-of-leaves absconding from the colony and making their own way back to England.

There were four such fellows who had also made their way to the Bank of Victoria at Ballarat on 14 October 1854. The bank on Bakery Hill was a wood-framed building clad with galvanised iron, known locally as the 'Iron Pot'.

The four robbers, John Bolton, Henry Garrett, Henry Marriott and Thomas Quinn, were all 'graduates' of Port Arthur. Their backs bore the marks of their education, and their ankles still bore the scars of the irons that once kept them at bay.

Quinn had travelled up from Geelong to join his old companions in their quest for riches, but did not want to be involved in the robbery if there was going to be any violence. They agreed to do their hold-up with unloaded pistols.

The four waited outside the building until closing time and, timing their entry just right, walked into the bank at the end of a good trading day. They waved their empty pistols at the tellers and offered to blow their brains out if any more than a whisper was raised.

The bank employees had their arms and legs 'fastened together like trussed fowls' and were forced to lie down on the floor while the bandits helped themselves to the open vault.

They got away with £18,000 in notes and gold, and headed for an abandoned shaft near the Gravel Pits.

After dividing up their ill-gotten gains, the gang split up and went their separate ways.

While this may have seemed the perfect crime – no one was hurt, no one was recognised and they all got away clean with a large sum of money – unfortunately for the gang, the cash had only been delivered to the bank by escort on the morning of the robbery. A dutiful clerk had already made a record of the numbers on this fresh delivery of crisp £50, £20 and £10 notes.

Garrett, like Gray before him, cut himself off from his companions. He travelled down to Port Phillip, sailed up to Sydney and boarded a ship for England. Marriott and Quinn carried their share down to Geelong in a covered wagon where they lay low for a while in a boarding house. The third burglar, Bolton, lay low in Ballarat.

The 'lady' of the boarding house was no longer enamoured of her husband. On hearing that a bank at Ballarat had just been hit, and observant of the manner with which her newly arrived guests liberally splashed their cash around, she waited for her moment.

Once her guests had gone out on a spree, she gave their room a once over. Finding the banknotes, nuggets, gold dust and coins under the floor covers, inside the mattresses, and in their swags, she saw an easy solution to her marital woes.

With her suitcase filled with loot and a male companion at her side, she was off, also to

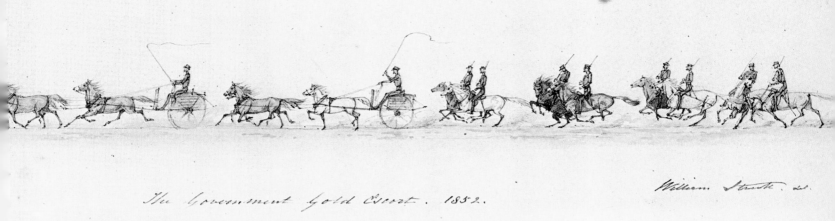

The Government Gold Escort. 1852.

William Strutt d.

Sydney. When the burglars returned to their room, they discovered to their surprise that someone else had been rummaging through their 'belongings'.

When the men inquired of their landlady and discovered that she too was missing, they put two and two together. Wisely, Marriott decided that the best thing to do was just to shut up; after all, they had been left with 'the biggest share of the cake'.

When the landlady attempted to pass a £20 note in Sydney, she was, unfortunately, in a tradesman's shop who had in his possession a list of the stolen notes. The Ballarat bank had quickly disseminated the list across the colonies. Not wanting to spend the rest of her days in prison, she spilled the beans, leading to the arrest of Marriott, Quinn and Bolton. By this time, Bolton was in Adelaide readying to board a vessel 'homeward bound'.

Deep Sinking, Ballarat, (lithograph by S.T. Gill, 1855)
Rex Nan Kivell Collection S3954, National Library of Australia, an6055917

Deep Sinking Ballarat

James J. Blundell & Co.
Melbourne

Panoramic view of Ballarat in the early 1850s
La Trobe Picture Collection, State Library of Victoria

Henry Garrett was already in London. Although **Scotland Yard** had received news of the robbery from a ship that had arrived a few days earlier, Garrett had cleverly come aboard on the pilot-ship before his vessel had docked.

The Eureka Gang

In June 1851, *The Geelong Advertiser* warned that 'large numbers of men – half bushranger, half goldseeker – are travelling along the roads robbing all who are unprotected'. They were attacking hopefuls heading for the New South Wales goldfields. By the end of the year, the same newspapers were warning of the huge number of '**t'other siders**' coming into the colony from Tasmania, attacking those on their way to the diggings.

John Baylie, Charles Bow, John Donovan, John Finegan and Henry Johnstone were such characters, and they adopted the name 'The Eureka Gang', sticking-up diggers on the road at Aitken's Gap to the north of Melbourne.

When they were eventually brought to ground, they stood accused of robberies all over the district. In court, one of the prisoners exclaimed in their defence:

'Here's one man says we stuck him up at Aitken's Gap, another at the Porcupine, another near Mount Egerton, and others at other places, and the police says they caught us in the Crown Hotel, Buninyong. Why, your honour, horses couldn't get over the ground in the time, what do you think we are, crows?' They were soon to be gaol-birds anyway!

He was in Regent Street one day when he heard a voice behind him cry out: 'Hullo Garrett, when did you arrive?' Some say that Inspector Webb had called out with the bush cry 'Coo-ee!', but whatever the cry, Garrett was caught unawares, turned and gave himself away. Taken back to his hotel, a large amount of the stolen property was discovered in his room. He was brought back to Melbourne to stand trial.

The four Ballarat bank robbers were each sentenced to 10 years hard labour. When questioned by counsel if he was in Geelong when the governor had arrived, Quinn answered, as quick as a flash: 'I don't associate much with governors except governors of gaols . . . I don't care much for their society.' Garrett was eventually granted a ticket-of-leave in August 1861, and he departed the colony for the goldfields in New Zealand, where he earned himself the honour of becoming that colony's first bushranger.

The account given here was recorded in Craig's *Adventures on the Goldfields*. There are, however, variations to the pattern of events. Some suggest that Marriott lay low in Ballarat for a while, and it was Quinn and Bolton who headed down to Geelong, then on to Melbourne where they sold their share to the London Chartered Bank in Collins Street.

From there they apparently went back to Geelong and then back up to Ballarat where Bolton was arrested after attempting to obtain a bank-draft for £1,450 from the very bank he had robbed only weeks earlier. When he passed his bundle of cash over the counter, the teller recognised the numbers and he was nabbed.

A Battle for Democracy, 3 December 1854

FROM THE BEGINNING OF THE GOLD rushes in both Victoria and New South Wales, thousands of people came from all over the world to try their luck and to make a fresh start.

Ships choked the harbours, many unable to sail away again as their crews abandoned them for the rush to the diggings. Across the former diggings there are countless Sailor's Gullies, Sailor's Creeks or Sailor's Flats that indicate the spot where these crews had slung their swag.

Sailors were treated much the same as convicted labour; they had very few rights to personal freedom and suffered the lash or the noose at the whim of their master.

These 'absconders' were joined on the diggings by hundreds of refugees from all the European wars. Add to this a liberal dose of Californian '49ers, topped off with boatloads of radical Irish lawyers and political activists, Scottish chartists,

Welsh orators, Wesleyan preachers, Catholic priests and hundreds of bolters from Tasmania, and the diggings were about to explode.

No longer could the colonial governors and the military commanders expect to rule with an iron fist and take from the digger as if the goldfields were their own. There were too many people on the diggings who didn't take to military rule or government decree; they demanded the right to live, work and die as they wished. These ordinary men were demanding to be treated as citizens — and democracy was a foreign concept to the English.

The government imposed a heavy licence fee on all those who were on the goldfields, whether or not they were there to dig. Many unfortunate 'diggers' were arrested just as they arrived. Those unable to pay were either 'chained to the logs', sometimes for weeks in all kinds of weather or sent to work on the roads. The government had

THE GOVERNMENT CAMP, BALLARAT, 1854.——TRO

not forgotten the value of enforced labour.

December 1851: Only weeks after the Victorian diggings had begun, over 14,000 attended an anti-licence protest meeting at the old shepherds' hut at Chewton on the Forest Creek goldfield.

August 1853: Following two years of constant bickering, petitioning the governor and altercations with the troops, a mass meeting was held in Bendigo. Thousands of armed diggers marched on the government camp, ready to do battle. They wore a red ribbon in protest, 'as a sign that those who wore it were pledged no longer to pay the licence fee.'

November 1854: One more year had passed with the government doing nothing but intensifying the frequency of licence hunts and creating dissatisfaction across the colony.

While the diggers were angry at the government's persistence with the licence fee, they also complained that they got little back from their taxes. They complained of the poor condition of the roads, the high cost of provisions, the treatment at the hands of the military, corruption of officials, and the lack of protection against bushrangers.

Into the middle of all this argument stepped yet another Irishman, Peter Lalor. On the morning of

FROM MELBOURNE. *From a Sketch by S. D. S. Huyghue.*

HON. PETER LALOR.

30 November 1854, he stepped upon a stump at the centre of a **stockade** built on the Eureka diggings. Beneath a fluttering blue banner emblazoned with a white cross and five white stars, in unison with the diggers massed before him, Lalor declared the diggers' oath: 'We swear by the Southern Cross to stand truly by each other, and defend our rights and our liberties.'

3 December 1854, just before dawn: The crude stockade that had been constructed around some tents with the fluttering blue flag at their centre was attacked by the troops of the 40th Regiment. In the short but vicious battle that ensued, 22 diggers were killed and six troopers lay dead or dying. Lalor had his left arm shattered with a musket ball and it was amputated in secret at the Presbytery of Father Smyth later that afternoon.

It was just like the days of Martin Cash and Donohoe 'The Wild Colonial Boy' with the Irish in the thick of the fight against the British authorities. Now they were aided by the gentlemen of 'the **California brigade**' who, with their glistening Colts tucked into their belts, were just as eager for a 'right royal tussle' as any old lag or bushranger.

While this battle was not of bushrangers against the police, it was the same battle against the same kind of injustice and prejudice that turned most good men against the law and the law-makers.

All of the leaders of the Ballarat Reform League (except Lalor who was kept hidden in Geelong) were brought to trial for **treason** under the watchful eye of the Protestant Irish judge, Redmond Barry, and in the end all were acquitted. The battle on Sunday 3 December 1854 may have been lost, but the war was eventually won.

The Storming of Eureka Stockade, 3 December 1854 (watercolour by J. B. Henderson)
Mitchell Library, State Library of New South Wales Collection

Bushrangers' Camp (watercolour by S. T. Gill, c. 1871)
La Trobe Picture Collection, State Library of Victoria

Horse Trading in the High Country — The Story of Bogong Jack

JOHN PAYNE (OR PAYNTER) remains an almost uncelebrated bushranger of the high country. The Kellys roamed the same inaccessible country as Payne decades after he had opened the route across the mountains from Gippsland.

Payne was born in Leicestershire, England, the son of John Griefotheran Payne, the prominent road and railway construction engineer who had served with the Duke of Wellington's army in the Peninsula War.

Young John Payne enjoyed a privileged childhood, but he was such an energetic and sporting young man that he seemed to spend almost as much time in the saddle as with his books.

He went up to Cambridge to further his opportunities, but again spent his time having fun — often riding horses. He joined the Cambridge Coaching Club, and it was an unfortunate incident while driving the mail coach on the Great North Road that led to his departure for Australia.

The appointed driver of the coach was asleep inside, taking the place of the young lady seated beside the carefree Payne. The horses, frightened by the noise of a passing steam-powered three-wheeled vehicle, reared up and the coach was overturned. Now, this was indeed an unfortunate accident for young John Payne. Although little damage had been done, the young lady, who suffered a broken collar-bone, was the daughter of a local squire with connections to parliament. It was across the squire's lands that the railways were hoping to run.

The squire insisted that John Payne had been spending far too much time in the pursuits of pleasures, including the pursuit of his daughter, and not enough time on his studies.

To avoid problems in the future prospects of the railways, Payne senior decided that it would be a good idea if Payne junior spent some time away from Cambridge and packed his son off to Australia.

In 1853, John Payne set out to London to kit himself out for his trip to Australia where he expected to find a position as a trooper in the gold escort company of the Port Phillip district.

While in London, Payne visited a Mr Barlow, the engineer of the Midland Railway, who was meeting with the great engineer of steel and steam, Thomas Brunel, at the time.

However, when he finally arrived in Port Phillip, Payne was dismayed to find that there was no position available for him with the gold escort. The persons with whom he had arranged letters of introduction had gone on to Port Jackson (Sydney).

He soon found his way around the town, enjoying the horse bazaar up the eastern end of Bourke Street where he had offers of work building fences up the bush. However, Payne was largely unused to any manual labour and was not keen to start.

By chance, he heard the landlord of Harper's Hotel, where he was staying, complain that his hotel roustabout had left for the diggings without warning and the job was up for grabs. John Payne was soon to be found up at six a.m., lighting the house fires, boiling the kettles for the servants, watering, feeding and grooming the horses, and cleaning the muddied boots of the hotel guests for £2 a week plus keep and 5/- tips. The landlord found it hard to believe that such a gentleman would take to such work, but this was just the first of many changes in the fortunes of young 'Jack'. Before long, however, he was advised of an opportunity to drive a mob of cattle brought down from Campbelltown in New South Wales to Omeo in the Victorian high-country where they

would be slaughtered to supply meat for the hundreds of miners there.

Payne jumped at the chance to get back into the saddle and be paid for it. He took to life in the bush with great relish, sleeping out under the stars with his saddle for a pillow.

It was not long before he became aware of the carelessness with which some cattle owners counted their herds. There was cattle wandering, often unbranded, across the high plains. The numbers arriving at the slaughtering pens would often be quite different to the numbers counted at departure. The cattle owners could do little to keep track of the situation, and trusted their drovers to furnish honest reports.

In 1856, John received a letter from Major General Sir Edward Nickle, commander of the 12th and 40th regiments at Port Phillip, offering him temporary command of the Castlemaine gold escorts. But John had made up his mind to join up with his mates, live a life free under the stars and make his fortune selling cattle. The only problem was that he didn't think that the cattle had to belong to him!

John disappeared into the bush and gradually began a highly profitable enterprise stealing Gippsland horses and driving them over the ranges to sell in the north. There were always horse-traders around the bustling goldfields of Beechworth, Yackanandah and Wangaratta, eager for a bit of prize Gippsland horse-flesh. The gang stole good horses from the north and drove them back over the ranges to sell to miners around the Omeo and Wood's Point diggings.

John Payne, now Bushman Jack, was popular wherever he went. He was quick-witted and charming, and had a repertoire of old coaching songs that entertained his fellow bushmen around the campfire or crowded pubs and rooming houses.

But it wasn't long before the police in Melbourne became concerned at the constant reports of stock losses, and a close eye was cast over the activities of all those seen going in and out of the mountains. Jack had developed an intimate knowledge of the bush, but even he was not able to control the events that surrounded him.

Two of his companions, George Chamberlain and William Armstrong, were planning to attack and rob a gold trader who was taking a case of gold worth £20,000 to the Gippsland coast. Jack wanted nothing to do with the robbery, he was, after all, a gentleman thief; a liberator of 'homeless' animals.

The robbery went ahead. Fifteen miles out of Omeo, the escort party for Cornelius Green, the gold trader, was attacked. The bandits opened fire on the escort and Green was killed, the trooper guarding the party was shot in the arm, and his horse bolted for the bush. A storeman was also wounded and a female in company with them was so traumatised that she was never able to give a coherent account of the affair.

When Green's body was recovered, his body had been mutilated. He had been shot through the chest, his skull smashed in with a tomahawk, his nose sliced off, and one hand almost cut from the arm. It seems that the thieves were angered that the horse carrying the gold had bolted for the bush.

Chamberlain and Armstrong were under suspicion of the murder of Green. A local storekeeper had seen them at the same lodging-house as Green and suspected that they may have learned of the gold escort. After the aborted attempt on the escort, they had stolen some good horses belonging to local farmers to make their escape. Although the local police reckoned that they could easily have covered 100 miles before the next day, it didn't take long before they were apprehended. Chamberlain and Armstrong were found hiding up a tree behind a shanty 50 miles from Omeo.

Both Sydney Penny and John Payne were also taken into custody, but they were later released.

Chamberlain and Armstrong were found not guilty of the murder of Cornelius Green, but of manslaughter and wounding, and were hanged, just the same, on 12 July 1859.

Jack tried to retire from his unlawful ways, but he was never forgotten. He was under constant surveillance, as much as could be maintained in the darkened, steep tracks of the heavily wooded high country. He was charged with horse-stealing several times, but remained free to roam his beloved mountains.

The facts of his demise are unknown. It is said that Jack was murdered while searching for gold near his hut at Mt. Fainter, but there were those who argued that this was unlikely as Bogong Jack was a 'horseman' not a 'prospector'.

A fellow who called himself 'Paddy Hekir' reported that he spent some time up in the high country with a man who would only identify himself as Jack.

Hekir apparently stayed in Jack's company for a while until one day he told some men in the Magpie Hotel at Beechworth that his mate Jack had been lost in the fog. They thought that Hekir must have been talking about Bogong Jack as no one had seen him around for a month or so.

A few months later, a prospector, after a few drinks, told how he had discovered a skeleton in a gully below a high cliff near Mt. Fainter. The back of the skull appeared as if it had been struck a blow from a miner's pick. The prospector had picked up a money belt hanging from a ti-tree and had found a gold sovereign not far from the body. He said nothing about the leather bag of sovereigns, the books in the pack saddle or the bundle of letters with a Leicestershire postmark that were also in the hut nearby.

The hut, once used by drovers and cattlemen, is used no more. It is rumoured that around midnight, a tall lean figure, booted and spurred, strides out from the tall timber and across the camp and holding yards, causing 'the cattle to leap to their feet and rush down the spur in terror'.

THE MURDER OF JOHN PRICE

IN 1854 JOHN PRICE was appointed as Inspector-General of Convicts in Victoria at a time when there was a rising demand for police services as thousands joined the rush for gold.

Prior to this, Price had been 'Civil Commandant for Norfolk Island', where his harshness had earned him the nickname 'The Monster of Norfolk Island'. Before then, he had been 'Muster Master of Convicts in Van Diemen's Land' where he had also earned a reputation for cruelty.

It was in Van Diemen's Land that the bushranger Martin Cash had suffered at Price's cruel hand, and Price's departure was welcomed by the convicts there.

Price's brutal reputation followed him to Victoria where many protested at his appointment.

There was such a demand for prisons at that time that Port Phillip Bay began to resemble the English ports before transportation. Ships were again turned into floating prisons, and some hardened and desperate men were 'rotting' in these hulks. It was the prisoners from the *Success* who brought an end to the career of Inspector-General Price. As he walked, unarmed, among them, the prisoners had downed tools in protest at the appalling conditions in which they were held, the less than adequate rations they received and the harshness of their labours at the Gellibrand quarries. Price demanded that they make their complaints 'in the proper form'.

Inspector-General John Price
La Trobe Picture Collection, State Library of Victoria

The men had had enough. One struck Price over the back of the head with a shovel, and the rest picked up the rocks they had been breaking and brought Price down. He was bashed and stoned to death by prisoners in the quarry at Port Gellibrand in March 1857. There were few who mourned his passing.

The prison hulk Success
La Trobe Picture Collection, State Library of Victoria

The Last of Their Kind

Governors Hack Their Way Into the History Books

The Outlaws:

New South Wales has at last got rid of the Breelong Outlaws. Jimmy Governor on October 28, was captured by a cluster of civilians who discovered the camp of the outlaw, and crept close to it, under cover of darkness. When they challenged the fugitive, he leaped to his feet, and ran like a deer, but was pursued, wounded and captured. Three days later in more daring fashion Joe Governor was shot dead ... this closes the most remarkable chapter of crime in Australian history.

— *REVIEW OF REVIEWS,*
20 NOVEMBER 1900

THE GROUP OF ABORIGINAL outlaws led by Jimmy and Joe Governor were the last of the bushranging gangs to be brought to justice at the beginning of the twentieth century. Joe Governor was an educated half-Aboriginal, well adapted to white society. He had worked as a police tracker and was a known horse-breaker. Jimmy, at the age of 23, had courted and wed a 16-year-old white girl, Ethel Page.

The women of the Breelong district were disgusted by this 'mixed marriage' and held Jimmy and his bride in deep contempt. They shifted out to a hut when Jimmy took a fencing job on the West Breelong property of pastoralist John Mawbey.

One day when Ethel came into Breelong for supplies, Mrs Mawbey and school teacher Helen Kurz abused her for marrying a black man and sent her away empty-handed.

Jimmy complained to Mawbey about this insult, and although Mawbey assured Jimmy that he and Ethel would have their supplies, the proud native man was still not satisfied.

Brooding over the insult to his bride, Jimmy and his mate, the half-blind Aborigine Jacky Underwood, decided to pay Mawbey a visit. They arrived one evening armed with an axe and a rifle – just in case. Mrs Mawbey opened the door and the men saw Helen Kurz standing alongside her. Jimmy asked for an apology, but instead he was ordered off the property. Helen Kurz added further insult to injury when she shouted: 'You black rubbish! You should be shot for marrying a white woman!'

Enraged by this remark, both Governor and Underwood attacked. There were the two women at the door and eight children inside when Jimmy and Jacky burst in. They struck first at Mrs Mawbey and Helen Kurz. The children, Grace and Percy, made a run for it, but they did not get far. Elsie Clark, a friend sleeping over, was also killed.

The attackers ran off into the night. When Mawbey was alerted by eight-year-old Bert, who had managed to escape the slaughter, he rushed into the house to find a bloody scene.

More than 2,200 police and civilians joined in the search for the murderers (by this time Joe Governor had also joined them on the run). Before they were captured, they managed to commit a further 80 crimes, from murder to robbery under arms. A reward of £1000 was offered as their pursuers began to close in on Jimmy and the boys.

After nearly four months, the trio's run was brought to an end. Jacky Underwood was the first to be captured and he was sent to prison to await his fate. Jimmy was peppered with buckshot as he lay sleeping on 27 October 1900, then captured and taken into custody. Joe managed to evade capture yet again.

On 30 October, John Wilkinson came upon Joe's campfire in the bush. Wilkinson crept forward signalling for his brother to join him. Although they had only one gun between them, the pair stepped out, surprising the outlaw and called on him to surrender. Joe made a dash for his rifle, but Wilkinson fired first. He missed and fired again, but he missed once more. Taking careful aim Wilkinson fired again, and Joe Governor was killed.

Jacky Underwood was hanged on 14 January 1901. Before Jacky was led to the gallows, he asked of the warder whether he would be in heaven in time for dinner. Jimmy was hanged four days later.

'THE CHANT OF JIMMY BLACKSMITH'

The 1985 movie *The Chant of Jimmy Blacksmith* was based on this story of Joe and Jimmy Governor.
The award-winning novel by Australian author Thomas Keneally was the inspiration for the film.

Glossary

bulwark — side of a ship that stands above deck, like a wall.

'California brigade' — armed men who had mining experience on the Californian diggings. Mostly Americans, their weapon of choice was the light Colt revolving-pistol.

carbine — a short rifle, usually issued to cavalry.

chain gangs — convicts sent to work, usually with a steel ball and shackles attached to their ankles, sometimes chained together to prevent escape.

consignor — person who had gone guarantor for the value of the gold, and paid the digger in advance of sale.

Crown, the — concept of ownership of, and allegiance to, the state that extends beyond politics.

emancipation — freedom. Once prisoners had served their time in the colonies; proved themselves worthy of release; or had rendered invaluable service to the government; they were freed and allowed to start a new life in the colonies.

mulatto — old-fashioned name for a person of mixed race. 'Black Douglas' was part African slave — from the West Indies — and part European.

musket — infantryman's gun, loaded by pushing powder and a single lead ball down the barrel with a long rod.

retribution — revenge.

Scotland Yard — home of the English Police Force.

sentinel — guard.

stockade — enclosed area, crudely constructed of poles or spikes driven into the ground. Usually built to keep convicts in overnight; the Eureka Stockade was built to keep the English army out.

't-other-siders' — ex-convicts from Van Diemen's Land (Tasmania). Another name for 'vandemonians' used by the ex-convicts themselves.

transportation — removal of prisoners from England to the colonies, where they were set to work as assigned labour.

treason — crime against the state, usually denial of allegiance to the state.

triangle — wooden structure to which prisoners were strapped to receive punishment by whipping.

vandemonians — ex-convicts, or escaped convicts, from Van Diemen's Land (Tasmania).

Index

Waverton Press
Level 1
100 Bay Road
Waverton NSW 2060
Australia
Email: publishing@fivemile.com.au

First published 2004
All rights reserved
© The Five Mile Press

Designed by Geoff Hocking

Printed in China

National Library of Australia Cataloguing-in-Publication data:

Hocking, Geoff.
Robbery Under Arms.
Includes index
For lower to middle secondary students.

ISBN 1 74124 095 6.

1. Australia - History - Juvenile literature.
I. Title. (Series: Australia in History).

994.02